Transport Helicopters

by Adele D. Richardson

Consultant:
Carl Shafer
Executive Director
American Helicopter Museum and Education Center

Bridgestone Books
an imprint of Capstone Press
Mankato, Minnesota

Bridgestone Books are published by Capstone Press
151 Good Counsel Drive, P.O. Box 669, Mankato, Minnesota 56002
http://www.capstone-press.com

Library of Congress Cataloging-in-Publication Data
Richardson, Adele D., 1966–
   Transport helicopters/by Adele D. Richardson.
   p. cm.—(The transportation library)
   Includes bibliographical references and index.
   Summary: Describes early models, major parts, and the workings of transport helicopters.
   ISBN 0-7368-0608-3
   1. Helicopters—Juvenile literature. [1. Helicopters.] I. Title. II. Series.
TL716.2 .R53 2001
629.133'352—dc21
                                                           00-022826

Editorial Credits

Karen L. Daas, editor; Timothy Halldin, cover designer and illustrator;
  Kimberly Danger and Heidi Schoof, photo researchers

Photo Credits

Corbis, 16
Defense Visual Information Center, cover
Index Stock Imagery 4, 18
Jason Hailey/FPG International LLC, 12
Richard Cummins, 6–7
Richard Laird/FPG International LLC, 20
Tom Caroll/FPG International LLC, 10

1 2 3 4 5 6 06 05 04 03 02 01

Table of Contents

Transport Helicopters

Helicopters move people and cargo. They can take off and land in small areas. Helicopters can travel to many places that trucks, airplanes, and trains cannot reach. Transport helicopters move cargo. They carry heavy objects in a sling.

sling

a strap-like object attached to the bottom of a helicopter

tail rotor blade

main rotor blades

landing skid

Parts of a Transport Helicopter

Transport helicopters have main rotor blades on top of the helicopter. Some transport helicopters also have a tail rotor blade. Rotor blades control the direction of the helicopter. Small transport helicopters have landing skids. Some large transport helicopters have wheels.

7

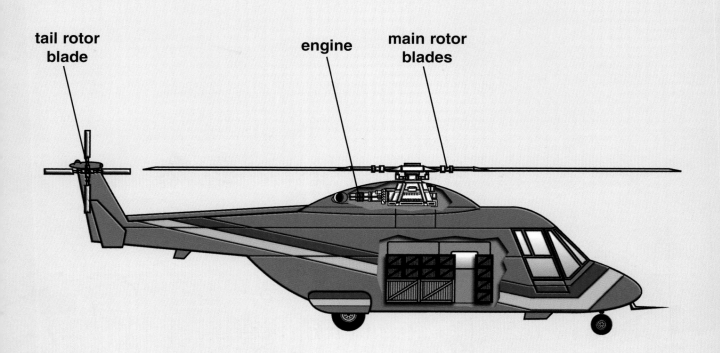

tail rotor
blade

engine

main rotor
blades

How a Transport Helicopter Works

A transport helicopter's engines burn fuel to create power. The power turns the rotor blades. The pilot uses controls to lift the transport helicopter off the ground. Transport helicopters can move in any direction or hover.

hover

to stay in one place in the air

Flying a Transport Helicopter

A pilot uses pedals, levers, and a stick to fly a transport helicopter. These tools control the movement of the rotor blades. The transport helicopter moves when the rotors tilt. The pilot watches gauges to make sure the helicopter is working correctly.

Before the Transport Helicopter

Trains, boats, trucks, and airplanes transported cargo before transport helicopters were invented. Trucks and boats traveled slowly. Trains only could travel to places that had train tracks. Airplanes only could take off from and land on runways.

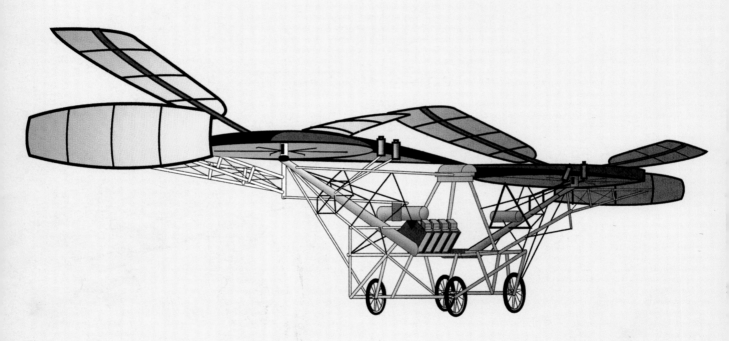

Inventor of the Helicopter

Paul Cornu invented the first helicopter
to hover. Paul was a French engineer.
On November 13, 1907, Paul made
the first piloted helicopter flight. The
helicopter hovered above the ground
for about 20 seconds.

Early Transport Helicopters

Igor Sikorsky invented the first successful helicopter. The *VS-300* made its first flight on September 14, 1939. In 1947, Frank Piasecki created the first heavy-lift helicopter. Today, people still build transport helicopters based on Igor's and Frank's designs.

Transport Helicopters Today

Helicopters deliver goods to places airplanes cannot reach. U.S. military transport helicopters often carry supplies to military ships. Some transport helicopters move goods from cargo ships to harbor docks.

military
the armed forces of a country

Transport Helicopter Facts

- Heliports are small airports. Only helicopters can take off and land at heliports.

- Some transport helicopters can lift objects as heavy as 125,000 pounds (56,700 kilograms). People sometimes use these helicopters to build tall buildings and bridges.

- Firefighters use transport helicopters to pour water on forest fires.

- Some ships have helipads. Transport helicopters land on these areas when they deliver cargo to ships.

Hands On: Build a Model Rotor Blade

A transport helicopter must have rotor blades to fly. You can build your own model rotor blades.

What You Need

Large index card
Ruler
Scissors
Paper punch
Pipe cleaner

What You Do

1. Carefully cut the index card to make a strip 6 inches (15 centimeters) long and 1 inch (2.5 centimeters) wide.
2. Punch a small hole in the center of the index card strip.
3. Fold the tip of the pipe cleaner.
4. Gently push the folded tip of the pipe cleaner into the hole. The pipe cleaner should fit tightly into the hole. The pipe cleaner and index card are your rotor blade.
5. Hold the rotor blade so the index card is at the top. Let go of the rotor blade. It will drop straight to the ground.
6. Twist the pipe cleaner between your thumb and finger so that the rotor blade is spinning. Let go of the rotor blade. It will twirl to the ground.

Words to Know

cargo (KAR-goh)—goods that are carried from one place to another

engineer (en-juh-NIHR)—someone who designs or builds machines

hover (HUHV-ur)—to stay in one place in the air

pilot (PYE-luht)—a person who flies a helicopter or other aircraft

rotor blade (ROH-tur BLAYD)—a long narrow wing that spins on top of a helicopter; a rotor blade lifts and controls a helicopter.

transport (transs-PORT)—to move people or goods from one place to another

Read More

Otfinoski, Steven. *Whirling Around: Helicopters Then and Now.* Here We Go! New York: Benchmark Books, 1999.

Oxlade, Chris. *Helicopter.* Take It Apart. Parsippany, N.J.: Silver Burdett, 1996.

Stille, Darlene R. *Helicopters.* A True Book. New York: Children's Press, 1997.

Internet Sites

American Helicopter Museum
http://helicoptermuseum.org
Canadian Museum of Flight—Kids
http://www.canadianflight.org/kids/index.htm
Helicopter Association International
http://www.rotor.com

Index